Original title:
Lost in the Larch Leaves

Copyright © 2025 Creative Arts Management OÜ
All rights reserved.

Author: Juliana Wentworth
ISBN HARDBACK: 978-1-80567-358-3
ISBN PAPERBACK: 978-1-80567-657-7

The Quieter Side of the Autumn Winds

Squirrels chatter as they dash,
Crispy leaves in a playful clash.
Winds whisper secrets, oh so sly,
While pumpkins giggle, passing by.

A crow attempts to steal a hat,
The farmer's cat just rolls on that.
Dancing shadows flicker and play,
What a silly, windy day!

Mosaics of Memory in the Archives of Nature

Colorful chaos, a jumbled cheer,
Nature's scrapbook, all gathered here.
Orange, yellow, brown—a swirl,
Leaves don't mind when they twirl.

A ladybug struts in polka dots,
Riding the breeze, forgetting thoughts.
With every gust, tales unfold,
Of sleepy naps in marigold.

A Passage Greener than Time Itself

Giddy strolls on a leafy path,
In the cool air, I feel the laugh.
Ducks wear hats, or so I swear,
While their reflections giggle in the air.

Skipping stones, one by one,
Each one splashes, but hey, that's fun!
Nature's bridges creak and sway,
Let's laugh and dance, come what may!

The Luminescence of Autumn Lullabies

Beneath the boughs, where shadows play,
A chorus of crickets starts their sway.
Crimson hues whisper in the night,
As owls hoot soft, a silly sight.

Sleepy bears in fuzzy coats,
Dream of honey and funny quotes.
Each twinkling star, a laughter shared,
In cozy nooks, the world is bared.

Memories Drift Amongst the Branches

Squirrels chatter, what a fuss,
Chasing shadows, just for us.
Nutty dreams in golden haze,
Nature giggles in bright displays.

Leaves are swaying like lost socks,
Tangled in the quirky rocks.
Roving through a leafy maze,
The woods are full of playful plays.

The Forgotten Path of Golden Foliage

Down the path that no one takes,
Where the wind sings, laughter wakes.
Crunching leaves beneath our feet,
Every step a silly beat.

Sunshine splatters here and there,
Bouncing beams without a care.
Frogs in hats hop with delight,
Chasing shadows in plain sight.

Veils of Amber in the Woodland Breeze

Breezes dance with puffy hair,
Whispers float through crisp, cool air.
Trees wear capes of amber glow,
Winking leaves put on a show.

Bugs are buzzing, what a song,
Messing up where they belong.
Branches wave and laugh in glee,
Like they're plotting mischief, free.

The Last Breath of Summer's Guardians

Bumblebees in fuzzy coats,
Stumbling home in little boats.
Ripe tomatoes laugh and roll,
On this merry, sunny stroll.

The sun dons shades, what a sight,
While butterflies take flight.
A final dance before the chill,
Nature's jesters, what a thrill!

The Trail Where Time Slumbers

A squirrel scurries, tail a blur,
Chasing acorns without a stir.
The path gets muddled, oh what a sight,
I trip on roots, oh what a fright.

Time ticks by in a goofy race,
Trees giggle softly, what a place.
Each step I take, I lose my pace,
Nature's humor: a cozy space.

Beneath the Glistening Veil

Fallen leaves like golden coins,
A carpet soft, where laughter joins.
I bounce through like a bouncing ball,
Hoping not to take a fall.

A robin laughs in chirps so bright,
While mushrooms dance, a funny sight.
These woods, they wink as I roam here,
Remind me too, don't shed a tear.

When Silence Falls in Golden Hues

The rustling leaves begin to creep,
In the quiet, the owls peep.
I'm giggling in a hushed ballet,
Dancing with shadows, come what may.

A pine cone drops, I duck in glee,
An acorn bounces off of me.
The silence breaks with nature's cheer,
I swear I heard a pine tree sneer.

Memories Wrapped in Crimson

A deer prances in a silly way,
Caught mid-leap, oh what a display.
My camera clicks, it stumbles too,
I chuckle hard, what will it do?

Colors swirl, a painter's mess,
Leaves are giggling, I must confess.
Wrapped in laughter, I skip and sway,
These fleeting moments, the sun's bouquet.

Leaving Footprints in Nature's Studio

In a forest where giggles play,
Dancing feet skip on the way.
Leaves rustle with a cheeky sound,
As I stumble, fall, just spinning 'round.

Nature laughs, a jolly friend,
Pine cones roll, the fun won't end.
My footprints sketch a silly line,
A canvas made, oh isn't it fine!

Chasing Shadows as Daylight Fades

Shadows stretch like playful cats,
As I try to outrun bats.
The sun dips low, the giggles grow,
I'm chasing whispers, where'd they go?

A tree stump waves as I pass by,
Or maybe it's just a friendly sigh.
Every shadow tries to tease,
In this twilight dodge, I find my ease.

The Alchemy of Foliage and Time

Leaves drop like coins in a wishing well,
Each one tells a tale to tell.
Turning green to gold so bright,
Nature's magic, what a sight!

I tried to catch one, spry and quick,
But it tickled me, what a trick!
With every step, I giggle and glide,
In this leafy world, my joy can't hide.

An Odyssey Through Gleaming Spheres

Bubbles float in autumn air,
I follow them without a care.
They pop! They fizz! A merry cheer,
Each burst a giggle, loud and clear.

Through branches, I jump with glee,
Dodging squirrels with reckless spree.
What joy in every leap and twirl,
A bubbly adventure, oh what a whirl!

Paintbrushes of Dusk and Dappled Light

The sun dips low, the sky wears pink,
Squirrels debate, should they fly or think?
Leaves twirl down in a dizzy dance,
While rabbits plot their evening prance.

The shadows stretch, a playful tease,
A raccoon giggles, sneaks toward trees.
Colors splash, like kids at play,
Nature's canvas at end of day.

Whispers of the Woods in Transition

Branches chatter in the cool night air,
The owl's wise grin, a knowing stare.
A fox prances, tail high with pride,
While the chipmunk's stash takes a wild ride.

Wind tickles leaves, a ticklish sound,
The woods are alive, twirls all around.
Each critter in sync, a comic troupe,
In nature's show, everyone's in the loop.

The Golden Hour's Reflection

Sunshine winks with a melted gold,
Ants in a line, their tales unfold.
Grasshoppers jump like they own the day,
While nature giggles in her own quirky way.

Reflecting laughs, puddles shimmer bright,
A badger's dance brings pure delight.
With friends all around, they join the fun,
In daylight's glow, the pranks just begun.

A Symphony of Nature's Farewell

Crickets join in with a squeaky song,
Bouncing off trees, where they belong.
The fireflies twirl, like small bright dreams,
While their glowing tails light up moonbeams.

Branches sway, as the choir grows loud,
A hedgehog nods, oh so proud!
Nature's tune, a hilarious show,
In the curtain's fall, all laughter flows.

Vibrations of Change Amongst the Trees

The trees sway, they dance so bold,
Whispers of secrets, new and old.
Branches shake with laughter, oh so bright,
While squirrels plot their acorn flight.

Colors burst, a clumsy display,
Leaves tumble down, making their play.
A gust of wind, they spin around,
Nature's jesters, forever unbound.

A Reverie in Saffron Hues

Golden leaves giggle in the breeze,
Tickling the branches, a rustling tease.
Sunlight winks at the playful sky,
While shadows plot how to fly high.

In saffron robes, they do ballet,
A clumsy twirl, then they sway.
Falling slowly, a comical race,
Landing softly, a leafy embrace.

Trails of Treasures Hidden in the Underbrush

Amidst the leaves, a treasure hoard,
Acorns, twigs—nature's reward.
A gopher stashes them with a grin,
Thinking these gems surely bring him win.

Mice join the feast, a wild gala,
Eating snacks like they're in a scala.
A leaf slips, creating a fuss,
And everyone laughs, causing a rush.

A Mosaic of Melancholy Leaves

Crimson and amber, they sigh and fall,
In this gallery, leaves have a ball.
Each one a story, a riot, a jest,
Feeling a bit like a weary guest.

They twirl in circles, a dance so grand,
Declining gracefully, as they planned.
Yet underneath, a humor brews,
As nature chuckles in vibrant hues.

Under the Gaze of the Observant Pines

Pines above point down their quills,
A squirrel juggles acorns, what a thrill.
While nature chuckles in rustling leaves,
A lizard's sunbath, like a prince he believes.

With every step, a twig snaps loud,
The trees all giggle, oh what a crowd.
A raccoon tips his hat, quite the charm,
While a doe gives a look, as if to disarm.

Journeying Through Nature's Kaleidoscope.

Colors swirl like a painter's dream,
Butterflies waltz, it's quite a scheme.
Crickets chirp in a chorus divine,
While bees buzz around like they own the wine.

Running through flowers, I trip on my shoe,
A patch of mud says, 'Hi there, boo!'
I laugh with the daisies, a silly brigade,
As the wind tells secrets, all wearing a shade.

Whispers Beneath the Canopy

Mossy whispers tickle my ears,
Squirrels gossip, sharing their fears.
A chipmunk makes faces, his cheeks are quite full,
With laughter that bounces, he swings like a fool.

The branches sway like a jolly old dance,
While butterflies flutter in a frolicsome prance.
Each rustle's a giggle, each shadow a grin,
In this forest of fun, where the wild things begin.

Shadows of the Evergreen Dance

Shadows waltz with a light-footed grace,
While a hedgehog rolls, it's a funny embrace.
The pine needles tickle, like fingers of glee,
With every new step, it's a wild jubilee.

Moss carpets the ground, a soft, squishy bed,
Where mushrooms wear hats, it's a party ahead.
I stumble and tumble; nature's joy is vast,
Each turn brings a laugh, oh, what a blast!

Shadows Like Echoes of Remembered Days

The squirrels are plotting, I swear,
With acorns and giggles, they scatter with flair.
Chasing their tails in a wobbly dance,
Nature's own circus, oh what a chance!

A raccoon in shades, sipping on tea,
He waves at the birds, says, "Join me, just see!"
The leaves whisper jokes, as they rustle around,
A comedy club where laughter is found.

Under the branches, a turtle in jest,
Claims he's the fastest, but we know the rest.
Ducks dressed in bow ties, quacking in tune,
These moments of joy, like a silly cartoon.

Yet here in the shadows, we're jamming along,
To the rhythm of nature, our own silly song.
So raise up your nuts, let's toast to the fun,
For every lost leaf, there's a new one to run!

Nature's Diary Written in Leaves

A leaf fell down with a thud and a grin,
It sighed, "I've seen things, oh where to begin?"
Grass blades are giggling, tickled by the breeze,
They dance in delight, with the highest of ease.

A chipmunk in stripes plays the role of the king,
While butterflies argue 'bout the best kind of bling.
The flowers are blushing, in colors so bright,
Gossiping 'bout sunbeams and nature's delight.

Each twig is a pen, writing tales of their day,
Of foxes who frolic and find time to play.
In the corners of woods, where mischief takes flight,
Nature's own diary, smiles left and right.

So gather 'round leaves, hear the stories unfold,
Of laughter and whimsy in hues of pure gold.
In this funny old world, where joy freely weaves,
Every tumble and slip leaves unforgettable leaves!

Journeying Through a Choreography of Colors

In a forest of colors, I prance and twirl,
My feet tickle the petals, oh what a whirl!
Each leaf sings a tune, as I skip with glee,
I trip over roots like a clumsy old bee.

The sun paints the sky with a silly grin,
While squirrels play tag and twirls begin.
I chase after shadows, they laugh and tease,
Saying, 'Catch us if you can, oh please!'

A Solitary Stroll in Yellow and Red

With a plucky hat and mismatched shoes,
I wander the paths, with all the hues.
Crimson leaves crunch beneath my feet,
Like chips in a movie, oh, isn't that sweet?

A whispering breeze tries to steal my snack,
I battle with nature, it's quite the smack!
As I dance around with a woeful pout,
These colors look like a rainbow's sprout.

Whimsical Woven Tales of Wilderness

Once a leaf claimed it was wise and old,
It whispered, 'Dear friend, I will share stories bold!'
But all it recounted were tales of the wind,
About dogs on surfboards and cats that pretend.

A rabbit burst forth, with a wig on its head,
It jiggled and laughed, and then quickly fled.
"Oh, look at me!" it squeaked with delight,
As I giggled and stumbled, trying to take flight.

The Dance of the Seasonal Spirits

The leaves waltz around like a carefree crew,
With acorns in tow, they know just what to do.
They spin and they leap, creating a scene,
As I join in the chaos, all silly and keen.

The sky tosses confetti, it's joyous and bright,
While clouds serve as dancers, what a funny sight!
I chuckle and flip, trying to take lead,
As nature gets giggly, fulfilling my need.

Underneath the Tumbling Canvas

Underneath the shabby sky,
A squirrel plotted, oh so sly.
With acorns gathered, in a pile,
He danced and twirled in cheeky style.

A crow cawed loud, with some great flair,
To join the fun, without a care.
Their antics made the trees go sway,
While branches waited for a stray.

The leaves, they fluttered, green and gold,
Whispered secrets, funny and bold.
A tumble down, like laughter's sound,
As nature's party spun around.

In every swirl, a chuckle shared,
With critters scheming, none prepared.
The sky turned blue with silly dreams,
Where laughter bubbled, floated streams.

Fluttering Heartbeats of the Wild

The bumblebees buzz with delight,
As they dance under the soft moonlight.
A hedgehog rolled, poking fun,
Claiming dusk was his time for a run.

The rabbits hopped without a care,
In silly circles, round and square.
Each leap a giggle, each skip a jest,
While daisies laughed, they felt the best.

The owls hooted with great surprise,
At squirrels wearing acorn ties.
'This looks ridiculous,' they would say,
Yet joined the fun, in their own way.

In moonlit mirth, the forest swayed,
With frolics that would never fade.
Each heartbeat thumped to nature's song,
As laughter echoed all night long.

The Light that Trickles Through

Sunbeams peeked between the trees,
Like tickles from a warm, soft breeze.
The shadows played hide and seek,
While giggles sprouted, oh so cheek!

A squirrel perched on a branch so high,
Wearing a wig, oh my, oh my!
He waved at friends down on the ground,
With a nutty grin that spun around.

The sun spun tales of whimsical ways,
As branches danced in golden rays.
The forest's laughter, a sweet refrain,
In every corner, joy did reign.

With every light that trickled down,
Silly stories wore their crown.
In every flicker, fun took flight,
Beneath the trees, the world felt bright.

Embracing the Cider-Scented Air

The breeze carried hints of sweet delight,
With whispers of apples, crisp and bright.
The trees were giggling, branches swaying,
In cider dreams, they were play-playing.

A bear in a hat, quite out of place,
Danced with joy, a silly grace.
The birds trilled tunes, quite loud and jolly,
As wind caught leaves in a merry folly.

Pumpkins chuckled, in their orange hues,
As they jived with sunlight's cues.
The ground covered in a patchwork quilt,
Of fallen leaves where fun was built.

In cider-scented air, they spun,
With playful spirits, all in one.
Each raindrop's patter, a playful dare,
In the forest's heart, nothing could compare.

The Unveiling of Autumn's Palette

As trees wear coats of amber flair,
Squirrels debate, their nuts laid bare.
One jumps high, misses the branch,
Has a momentary, acorn dance.

Chirps and caws fill the chilly air,
While birds glance down, a curious stare.
A leaf flutters, bold, like a show-off,
A gust of wind gives it a toss.

Rabbits hop, oh what a sight,
Piles of leaves make a soft flight.
One lands smack in a puddle's giggle,
Bouncing back with a mud-splattered wiggle.

Pine cones play hide and seek here,
With antics that make us all cheer.
In this painted park, we laugh and chase,
As autumn unveils its golden grace.

Encounters at the Crossroads of Change

Two paths cross where murmurs dwell,
One leads to chaos, just like a spell.
The other? A quiet place to rest,
Where a fox claims he's the best dressed.

A crow squawks tales of seeds galore,
While a lone turtle forgets to explore.
Bumbling through leaves, a goat appears,
Wearing shades, drinking imaginary beers.

At the bend, a deer strikes a pose,
Starts a dance, while no one knows.
A rabbit joins, adds a hop or two,
And suddenly, it's a furry review.

As the sun dips low, shadows play,
Critters mingle in a merry display.
Every twist a comic spree,
At this crossroads of absurdity.

Dreaming in the Gold of Decaying Leaves

In a pile of foliage, dreams collide,
A raccoon snoozes, nowhere to hide.
He dreams of fish and midnight snacks,
While a wise owl completes the hacks.

Bright yellow leaves tap-dance down,
Swirling 'round the village clown.
He juggles acorns, makes a splash,
As geese waddle by, giving a flash.

A hedgehog stirs, presses repeat,
Waking to find his cozy seat.
With a yawn, he stretches wide,
Leaves stick like trophies, his autumn pride.

The scene unfolds, a giggling game,
Each critter's antics a bit insane.
In the golden glow of nature's tease,
We laugh at life among the trees.

A Memorable Journey Through Falling Petals

Petals swirl in the crisp, brisk air,
A stray dog chases without a care.
He sniffs a bouquet, takes a grand leap,
But trips on a vine, falls in a heap.

Chirpy chicks, peeking from a nest,
Ready to watch the world at its best.
They squawk and slip, lose their perch,
Landing smack in a neighboring church.

A butterfly flutters, a fragile jest,
Sipping from flowers, full of zest.
But misses a petal, spins around,
Lands on a snoozing cat, quite profound.

Through all the laughs and little blunders,
Nature's stage plays sweet wonders.
In falling petals, pure delight,
Every misstep's a comic flight.

The Ethereal Flicker of Leafy Ghosts

In the wind, they dance and twirl,
Sassy sprites in a leafy whirl.
Whispers of colors, orange and gold,
Giggling secrets, stories untold.

One snagged my hat, oh what a sight!
Chasing shadows, now we take flight.
They laugh like children, wild and free,
Playing tricks, much to my glee.

I stumbled and fell, into a pile,
Leaves danced around with cheeky style.
"Catch me! Catch me!" they seemed to say,
As I tripped and laughed, all in the play.

But as dusk painted the world with haze,
The ghostly leaves begun their phase.
Flickering softly, fading away,
In a rustling whisper, joy led astray.

Captive in the Hues of Dusk

Beneath the branches, playful and spry,
I found a hue I can't deny.
Greens turned gold, in a silly twist,
Under dusk's palette, I just can't resist.

A squirrel winked, then sent me a tease,
His acorn stash swaying in the breeze.
I thought of joining his vibrant quest,
But he dashed away, so much for rest!

The shadows grew long, as chuckles rang,
Even the owls joined in with a clang.
Trying to catch a laugh in the air,
But ended up stuck in a leaf-laden chair.

As giggles echoed, the sun took a bow,
I waved goodbye to the night's leafy crowd.
In a world of colors, I learned to play,
In the hues of dusk, we dance 'til the day.

Fragments of October's Remnants

Oh, October, you sly little sprite,
With your confetti of leaves, such a sight.
Dancing on sidewalks, in breezy delight,
You make me chuckle at your bold invite.

"Catch me if you can!" a bright leaf cries,
As I tumble and fumble, under clear skies.
In a game of tag, I fall on my face,
And the leaves all giggle, what a clumsy race!

A cartwheel of colors spins 'round my way,
With fragments of laughter, come join the play.
Just when I thought I could pull off a trick,
A gust of wind sends my plans in a flick!

In the chaos of charm, I find my own groove,
With every slip, it's a chance to improve.
For October's remnants, all cheerful spree,
Brought a smile to my heart, so wild and free!

The Twilight Tangle of Swaying Sprigs

In twilight's glow, sprigs start to sway,
Whispering secrets, come join the fray.
A merry dance of the branches and leaves,
Each twirl and twist, a jest that deceives.

"Step lightly!" they call with a rustle and cheer,
As I sidestep cautiously, wracked with fear.
The trunk curtsies, the branches elude,
While I stand bewildered in leafy shrewd.

They gather 'round with a mischievous plot,
Binding my feet, with a giggle and knot.
No escape from this tangled affair,
Leaves throwing laughter high in the air.

Yet under the stars, the laughter ignites,
Swaying sprigs show off their joyful sights.
We'll dance 'til the moon joins the fun as well,
In a twilight tangle, where stories dwell.

The Rustle of Forgotten Stories

Underneath the twirling shades,
Squirrels plot their autumn raids.
Chasing tales of acorn gold,
Whispers of the bold and old.

A chipmunk sings a silly song,
Of leaves that flutter all day long.
Mice giggle in their leafy beds,
While puzzled owls shake their heads.

Gusty gales with playful grunts,
Tickle trees in silly stunts.
Branches sway and wave goodbye,
To pesky crows that soar on by.

In the rustle, laughter weaves,
As jokers hide among the leaves.
Nature's comedy unfolds,
With stories waiting to be told.

Embracing the Fall's Gentle Breath

Breezes kiss the frolic path,
As leaves engage in gentle math.
Counting hops of froggy friends,
Whiskers twitch as summer ends.

Pumpkins roll with much delight,
Scaring crows in playful fright.
A mischievous raccoon sneaks,
Amongst the crunch of autumn tweaks.

Chirps of crickets shake the air,
As friendships bloom with leafy flair.
Hiccups from the bubbling brook,
Join the laughter in the nook.

With every twirl the trees behave,
Dancing leaves, no hearts to save.
Swaying to the autumn's tune,
Even squirrels take up the croon.

The Forest's Tapestry of Change

In a quilt of gold and brown,
The forest dons its finest crown.
Bumbling bees in hats so grand,
Buzz with secrets of the land.

A fox in flannel plays the sly,
Winks at rabbits hopping by.
Tails flick as they skip along,
Footprints marking nature's song.

Amongst the leaves, a party brews,
Frogs bring snacks; the owls bring blues.
Chipmunks break into a dance,
While trees sway, lost in a trance.

Every leaf a story told,
Of laughter shared and adventures bold.
The forest spins a yarn so bright,
Of whimsical joy in autumn's light.

Navigating the Winds of Transition

Rustling whispers, secrets float,
Through branches that dance and gloat.
Chubby cheeks and toes that freeze,
Chipmunks giggle in the breeze.

With every gust, the games ignite,
Leaves setting sail in a wild flight.
Dancing as if in a race,
Oh, how the crunches tickle their face!

The maples stare with fiery flair,
While acorns tumble through the air.
A hedgehog rolls like a tumbleweed,
Chasing dreams of snacking greed.

Yet midst the fun, a solemn thought,
Change arrives, but not for naught.
For every twist and spin we find,
A treasure trove for hearts and mind.

Echoes of Autumn's Embrace

In the woods where laughter plays,
Leaves do pirouettes in a blaze.
Squirrels gossip, nuts in their grip,
Chasing shadows on a joyful trip.

Beneath the trees, a hidden dance,
Every twist is pure romance.
The acorns chuckle, rolling down,
While critters prance in leafy gown.

With each gust, a giggle sweeps,
Nature's whispers, secrets peep.
Owl in spectacles, wise and spry,
Winks at the moon, oh my, oh my!

In this meadow, cheer's to find,
Nature's quirks, they're one of a kind.
So come and twirl amidst the fun,
Where autumn sings and smiles run.

Tangles of Time in Treetop Dreams

Up in the branches, dreams take flight,
With every leaf, a giggle bright.
Chipmunks debate who's winning the race,
While crows crack jokes at a squirrel's face.

A flutter here, a rustle there,
Leaves comically trap all unaware.
Ticklish breezes make the trees sway,
Creating laughter in their ballet.

Pinecones tumble like clumsy clowns,
As daylight wanes and the sun frowns.
Nature's whimsy, a constant tease,
In tangled branches, life's a breeze.

So let us dance along this way,
Among the branches, we'll laugh and play.
For in these tangled tales, we see,
The funny side of harmony.

Rustling Secrets in the Forest's Heart

Whispers carry on the autumn air,
Leaves are giggling, full of flair.
A raccoon grins with a pie on his lap,
While hedgehogs argue in a grassy gap.

Beneath a canopy of golden hues,
Frogs sing ballads in silly shoes.
Wandering rabbits, tails in a swirl,
Chase their own shadows, here we twirl.

Mushrooms pop up with such a cheer,
Giggles echo, we gather near.
The laughter rolls like ripples wide,
In nature's heart, where joy can't hide.

So take a seat amongst this cheer,
With every rustle, let's draw near.
In secret glades, the humor soars,
As autumn's spirit forever roars.

Where the Pine Needles Weep

Underneath the pines, oh what a scene,
Needles fall like jokes, crisp and keen.
A porcupine dances without a care,
While birds above chuckle in the air.

Laughter echoes through boughs so tall,
In this woodland, we all stand tall.
Sapsucker plays on a drum of bark,
As even the dark gives a chuckling spark.

Mistletoe giggles, a lover's tease,
While raccoons toast to the autumn breeze.
Such merriment in each rustling leaf,
Spraying joy like a playful thief.

So join the fun, let the chuckles flow,
In the land where needles softly glow.
Among the pines, let laughter reap,
For even trees have secrets to keep.

Whispers of Autumn's Embrace

In shades of gold, the squirrels plot,
Their acorns hidden, oh, such a lot!
With little twitches, they dance around,
In this leafy maze, they are glory-bound.

The branches creak with secret laugh,
As if they share a cheeky path.
A crow caws out, 'You can't be serious!'
While bugs are planning their grand delirious.

The breeze tickles leaves, they giggle in flight,
As if to tease the fading light.
Around they swirl, a colorful fright,
Spreading joy in a frolicsome night.

Oh, autumn, you trickster in nature's game,
Turning the woods into a circus fame.
With every rustle, a chuckle will rise,
In this whimsical world, we're all in disguise.

Secrets Beneath the Needle Carpet

Underneath the pine, critters engage,
In a wild, silly autumn stage.
Frogs tell tales in croaks and ribbits,
While ants throw parties, sans any limits.

Mice don hats made of pine needles,
Swirling in circles, all dizzy with deeds.
A hedgehog winks with a spiky grin,
Announcing loudly, 'Let the fun begin!'

Butterflies giggle in twirls so bright,
Chasing shadows, dancing in flight.
Whispers of laughter, they flutter about,
In this needle carpet, there's no room for doubt.

With every step, the earth gives a creak,
The forest chuckles, what a cheeky peak!
Secrets abound in this playful trek,
Under needle canopies, life's a speck!

A Dance with the Amber Shadows

In twirls of amber, shadows prance,
The trees hold hands in their leafy dance.
A chipmunk twirls with a jaunty hat,
While singing to bugs, 'Imagine that!'

The moon peeks through with a giggle so bright,
As the stars all join in, what a sight!
Twirling with glee, they chase their tails,
Through tangled branches and winding trails.

Laughter erupts as leaves take flight,
Like confetti falling, what a delight!
Echoes of merriment bounce low and high,
As critters create their own lullaby.

Oh, dance, sweet shadows, in autumn's cheer,
With every chuckle, we hold you dear.
In this playful scene where nature unfolds,
A story of laughter forever told.

Echoes of a Fading Canopy

The canopy whispers, 'What's your plan?'
As branches wave to create a fan.
Leaves scatter down in a jolly parade,
As squirrels slip by, all mischief displayed.

Each echo ricochets, full of jest,
'There goes the wren; she thinks she's the best!'
Her tiny voice shrieks as she claims her throne,
While the trees hold back their giggles grown.

The breeze joins in, tickling the ground,
While the mushrooms pop up with glee all around.
'We're in costume!' they bob and sway,
In this fading world where laughter will play.

So raise a toast to the brisk autumn air,
As the whispering woods lend us their care.
With hidden chuckles and warm, silly hugs,
Nature's grand stage for all its little bugs!

Leaves of Light in a Brisk Twilight

In a swirl of gold and rust,
Squirrels play hide and seek,
One hides in a dancing bush,
But it's just a little sneak.

The branches shake with giggles,
As winds tickle their feet,
A fallen leaf slips down,
And lands on a bird's seat.

Beneath the twilight's glow,
A raccoon breaks into dance,
He thinks he's quite the star,
In this leafy, silly prance.

Nature throws a grand ball,
With twirls of every hue,
The trees snicker in whispers,
As they watch the fun ensue.

Cadence of the Cascading Canopy

There's rhythm in the branches,
A funny little sway,
As chipmunks strike a pose,
To show off in the fray.

A leaf glides through the air,
And lands on the dog's head,
He thinks he's wearing fashion,
In colors bright and red.

Beneath a quilt of colors,
A foolish crow does tease,
He shouts out silly verses,
And chuckles through the breeze.

The sun dips into shadows,
As laughter fills the scene,
In this playful canopy,
Life dances evergreen.

Cinders of Change in a Green Fire

Amidst the crunch of crispy hues,
A hedgehog rolls with flair,
He thinks he's in a race,
But he's just rolling bare.

A gust lifts up a dandy hat,
On the head of a prancing hare,
He hops around in style,
With leaves that swirl in air.

A comical squirrel just can't seem,
To find the right direction,
He zigzags through the foliage,
With utmost mis-con-nect-ion!

As night drapes down the forest,
The silly critters fade,
But tomorrow brings more laughter,
In this leafy masquerade.

The Surrender of the Sundering Woods

The woods begin to rumble,
With critters bold and brash,
A raccoon dons a crown of leaves,
And claims to be quite posh.

The branches sway with laughter,
As shadows dance around,
A turtle taps his tiny feet,
To a non-existent sound.

A leaf slips from the treetops,
Plops right on the bear's snout,
He blinks in sheer confusion,
And gives a big loud shout.

In this surrender of the woods,
A silly tale unfolds,
Nature's choir sings with joy,
In twirls of red and gold.

The Whispering Woods at Dusk

Beneath the trees, I trip and tumble,
Where echoes laugh, and shadows fumble.
A raccoon stole my snack, oh dear!
I'll keep my secrets, shh, don't leer!

The owls hoot jokes, they're quite the crowd,
As squirrels chatter, feeling proud.
The moon peeks in, a cheeky grin,
While I'm convinced the trees have kin!

I dance with night, in a goofy spin,
A deer stares back, amused within.
I bow and twirl, my footsteps loud,
The forest giggles, I'm so very proud!

An Odyssey of the Overlooked

In a thicket thick, I found a sock,
Its partner gone, a cruel clock.
I ponder life, where did it roam?
Maybe it's off to find a new home!

Bugs flutter by, in tiny trains,
Carrying snacks for their dinner gains.
I wave hello, they zoom away,
Do they all have plans for the day?

The groundhog laughs, with crumbs on his cheeks,
Says my lost shoe is what he seeks.
He points at fungi, that look like hats,
I swear they're plotting with the cats!

Patterns of the Passing Season

Autumn leaves swirl, like a wild ballet,
They tickle my nose, then dance away.
A pumpkin slips, it's gone with a thud,
Oops! A splatter, here comes the mud!

Frolicking foxes play hide and seek,
They leap and prance, so spry, so sleek.
I try to join, but trip on a twig,
Fall in the leaves, oh mighty big!

The colors clash, like clothes from the past,
Each shade a story, a contrast cast.
Laughter erupts, from tree to tree,
The forest's alive, come laugh with me!

Secrets Etched in Shades of Bronze

Whispers in whispers, the trees conspire,
As leaves' gold secrets spark my desire.
I wonder what tales the bark could tell,
Of squirrels with acorns who wish me well!

A chipmunk scolds, "You're in my space!"
I raise my hands, "Just admiring grace!"
He puffs up proud, then dashes on by,
A speedy escape, that little guy!

With every crunch, a story unfolds,
In vibrant hues, a treasure of golds.
I couldn't help but giggle and cheer,
The woods here are filled with beings dear!

Beneath the Boughs of Whispered Time

Under boughs where shadows play,
Squirrels dance in bright ballet.
Chasing tails and acorns round,
Laughter echoes, sweet and sound.

Tangled vines, a maze of cheer,
Who knew trees could bring such gear?
With every trunk a new delight,
A forest stage, all day and night.

Roots like legs that stretch and crawl,
Do they trip or just enthrall?
Jumps and hops, they have no care,
Nature's jesters everywhere.

So let us join this leafy jest,
In timbered glee, we find our quest.
With chuckles shared and smiles wide,
In lush embrace, let fun abide.

Enigma Wrapped in Nature's Bounty

In this grove, a riddle hums,
As branches sway and nature drums.
Where whispers weave a playful tale,
And branches twist like a goofy snail.

The mushrooms giggle, oh so sly,
Winking at the clouds up high.
Underneath, the birds convene,
Mimicking laughs, a feathered scene.

Bouncing bees with busy flair,
Trip the light, without a care.
Pollinating with a buzz and wink,
Nature's jesters starting to think.

So don your hat made of the sun,
Join in on this hidden fun.
For every leaf beneath the sky,
Holds secrets sweet that make you sigh.

Sentinels of Solitude

Stately trees with leafy scarves,
Watching all with silent laughs.
Each branch a hand that holds a smile,
Though standing still, they host their style.

Nature's guards, with trunks so stout,
They watch as critters scurry about.
With every breeze, they sway and tease,
Rustling jokes among the leaves.

Sitting here, I ponder why,
The tallest trees refuse to fly.
Maybe heights are just for show,
While whispers chuckle down below.

So raise a toast to roots so deep,
As branches shake and secrets seep.
For in this grove of quirky sights,
We find the joy of silly flights.

A Tapestry of Fading Green

In the woods where autumn calls,
Leaves like laughter gently fall.
Each hue a grin, a playful tease,
Dancing down on the autumn breeze.

Branches creak with slight disdain,
At squirrels acting very vain.
Running wild in leafy bliss,
Chasing shadows, what a twist!

Nature's quilt, a patchwork bright,
Stitches of glee in fading light.
Every shade tells a silly tale,
Of woodland pranks that never pale.

So gather round this colorful scene,
With glee we wander through the green.
For laughter's found in every hole,
In this wild, whimsical stroll.

Time's Tattered Map of Decay

A squirrel with a flair, up high in the tree,
He's holding a map, but it's covered in brie.
With crumbs on his paws, he makes quite the mess,
He claims it's a treasure, I must confess.

The branches all shake, as he jumps all around,
Chasing after dreams that are stuck on the ground.
Leaves tumble like coins, a soft, leafy rain,
While the wind whispers secrets of unclaimed domain.

He scribbles his notes with a flourish and cheese,
Declaring this forest the land of the freeze.
But what does he find? Just some acorns and bark,
Yet he dances and twirls, a true adventurer's lark.

So here's to the map that's distorted by fun,
In a world where the squirrels play tag with the sun.
Through giggles and glances, we gather today,
Time's tattered map shows us how to play.

Melodies of Faded Flora

The petals all groan with a giggle and twist,
As if they remember a time that they missed.
A daisy sings off-key, but brave in her song,
While roses roll eyes, it's a whole lot wrong.

The wind throws a dance, a beat that is wild,
While daisies and violets get silly, beguiled.
In laughter they sway, what a curious sight,
A floral performance that lasts through the night.

The moss plays the drums, in the hum of the air,
While bushes recite tales of whimsical fare.
As snails join the show, with a swagger so slow,
Each leaf is a note in the green, leafy flow.

So join in the laughter, let life serenade,
In melodies sung where no character fades.
Amid faded flora, we revel and cheer,
For nature's a stage, and the fun is right here.

Pondering Among the Fallen Spheres

A ponderous chipmunk, with eyebrows askew,
Stares hard at a pinecone, like it has a clue.
It's not just a snack, it's life's greatest prize,
But that furry little fellow's lost in his sighs.

The wind rolls the leaves, they dance on the ground,
As if they're debating what wisdom they've found.
An acorn falls plump, with a thump, and a roll,
While critters conspire, seeking grandiose goals.

A hedgehog joins in, with a hat made of leaves,
Proclaiming it's fashion that no one perceives.
He struts with great care, on the trails they have made,
As squirrels gaze wide-eyed, in bewildered charade.

So let's muse a bit longer, in this leafy retreat,
Among fallen spheres, where misguided hearts meet.
For laughter is plenty, and wisdom runs low,
In moments like this, we let go of the woe.

The Last Waltz of the Canopy

The trees are all swaying, in their evening gown,
With branches like arms, they twirl all around.
Each leaf is a partner, in a dance so bold,
While critters and shadows share stories untold.

A woodpecker taps, keeping beat with the breeze,
As night serenades, and brings whispers with ease.
A squirrel flips grapes that a raccoon has tossed,
In this canopy ball, no one counts the lost.

The moon peeks down, in her silvery dress,
As owls hoot like drummers, a feathery mess.
Each rustle and crackle is part of the fun,
As the last waltz unfolds 'neath the stars one by one.

So raise up your glasses of dewdrops and cheer,
For the dance of the forest, with all who are near.
In laughter and music, let nature enthrall,
The last waltz of the canopy won't end at all.

Enchanted by October's Veil

Among the gold beneath my feet,
I tripped on leaves, oh what a feat!
The squirrels chuckled, branches swayed,
As I danced clumsy, unafraid.

I thought I saw a wizard's hat,
But it was just a massive rat!
With wand of acorns, how absurd,
I bowed to nature, felt a bird.

A fairy waved, or was it me?
My laugh echoed, wild and free.
The trees whispered, "Dance a jig!"
I stomped around, but sprained a twig.

As shadows creeped from dusk to night,
I left behind my goofy fright.
With giggles echoing in the air,
Autumn's magic, everywhere!

A Sigh at the Edge of the Wood

At the path's end, I did declare,
"How did I end up sitting here?"
The mushrooms laughed, with caps so round,
I thought they'd dance upon the ground.

A hedgehog passed, gave me a glance,
I tried to join his little dance!
My footing slipped, a tumble, oh dear,
The nearby trees erupted in cheer!

With twigs now tangled in my hair,
I wobbled home, without a care.
The moon giggled, stars joined in,
I wondered where this day had been.

When dawn broke through the trembling light,
I waved goodbye to silly night.
The woods would whisper tales so fine,
Of mishaps and laughter, all mine!

Shades of Memory Beneath the Pines

Beneath the pines, I found a hat,
A sleepy owl just sat and sat!
I wore it askew, feeling so grand,
While squirrels plotted their mischief planned.

A raccoon peeked, giving a nod,
"Join us, friend, it's a tad odd!"
With hoots and prowls, we danced in glee,
A woodland shindig, wild and free!

The trees started swaying, slow and low,
I tried to lead but stepped on toes.
With laughter ricocheting through the air,
I flailed and spun, without a care!

As twilight draped its velvet cloak,
The creatures sighed, "Oh, what a joke!"
We parted ways, with chuckles free,
I'll never forget this jubilee!

The Aria of Falling Fronds

In a sonnet of leaves, I began to twirl,
With fronds as my partner, oh what a whirl!
The wind laughed loud, it took my hand,
As we spun together across the land.

The ground was littered with autumn's gold,
Each step a classic, never too bold.
A butterfly joined, with delicate grace,
Together we laughed in this joyous space.

A crow cawed loud, "Stop the show now!"
But I was too busy for such a bow.
With fronds like confetti, I took a dive,
In this wonderful moment, I truly thrived.

As evening fell, and shadows grow,
I whispered thanks to this autumn show.
With each giggle curling in the breeze,
I danced with delight amongst the trees!

Murmurs of the Grounded Conifers

In the woods, the trees all jest,
Telling tales of their leafy quest.
Squirrels dance in absurd delight,
While rabbits giggle, what a sight!

Pine cones plop like ping pong balls,
The laughter echoes through the halls.
Branches sway, they're having fun,
Nature's party has just begun!

The roots beneath are tickling feet,
Prompting everyone to skip and leap.
With rustling leaves that laugh along,
It seems the forest sings a song!

So if you wander where woods are deep,
Join the merriment; don't just peep.
The ground is giggling, and you should too,
In a world where the silly blooms anew!

The Uncertain Pulse of Nature's Heart

A frog croaks out a worried tune,
As bees buzz round like mini balloons.
Nature's heart beats fast and slow,
Petals shimmy, saying, "Whoa!"

The clouds are in a playful race,
Each one dodging with silly grace.
A daisy trips on a ferny friend,
While laughter floats on the blustery end.

Everything's quirky; trees tease the sun,
Whispering secrets, oh, what fun!
The river giggles, splashing about,
While fish tell tales of their latest rout.

In this dance, chaos rules the day,
Where the wind says, "Come and play!"
Amidst the pulse of nature's cheer,
You can't help but join in here!

Tranquility Amidst a Tangle of Branches

Beneath tangled limbs, calmness brews,
While squirrels debate the best tree views.
A twisty path leads to a sigh,
As foliage flutters, waving bye!

Amidst the chaos, a chipmunk grins,
Count how many acorns he wins.
Branches tickle, petals spin,
In this peaceful mess, laughter begins!

With roots that tangle like childhood games,
The forest whispers, "Who needs names?"
In such a riot, serenity's found,
As playful echoes swirl all around.

Come join the fun in wild repose,
Where tranquility juggles and giggles grows.
Amidst those branches, let's get loose,
In nature's giggle, there's no excuse!

Fleeting Moments on a Forest Path

On a path where shadows mix,
Footsteps tap a rhythm, a little fix.
Birds chatter with their silly charms,
While flowers dance, waving their arms.

As I stroll through this leafy maze,
A worm does a wiggle, such silly ways.
The sun peeks in with a cheeky grin,
While nature grumbles, "Let the fun begin!"

A sudden rustle, a deer makes a dash,
"Come back!" I shout, but they're gone in a flash.
Leaves giggle softly, the breeze takes a breath,
In this moment, I forget about death.

With laughter echoing through the trees,
Each tiny tickle brings me to my knees.
The forest plays tricks, jokes, and glee,
In fleeting moments, I feel so free!

Canvas of Dreams and Decay

In a park where colors clash,
The squirrels wear hats made of trash.
Frogs jump high with a song in their throat,
While a single leaf tries hard to float.

Brush strokes fade as the sun dips low,
A painter with paintbrushes in tow.
He spills his colors, yells with glee,
"Who needs a canvas? Just look at me!"

With each laugh, the trees start to sway,
As branches whisper, "What a weird day!"
The wind joins in with a playful twist,
Nature's own jester, too fun to resist.

So let's dance and spin in the golden glow,
With roots that wiggle and branches that grow.
A gallery bursting with silly delight,
Where dreams drift by, both awkward and bright.

The Hush of Seasonal Change

When autumn arrives, the world wears a grin,
Leaves chatter softly, "Let the games begin!"
A pumpkin decides it wants to roll,
While a snail claims it's the king of the shoal.

The wind swirls in, playing tricks on the trees,
Tapping their shoulders, saying, "If you please!
Show me your moves, I'm a dance champion!"
But the trees just sigh, "We're not ready, man!"

Nuts drop down like confetti from above,
The critters all scramble, it's a nutty love.
A hedgehog slips on an acorn in stride,
And falls on a cozy leaf pile of pride.

Yet among all the giggles and gentle air,
A shy little seed wonders what's fair.
"Will I grow tall or just stay a snack?"
The laughter grows louder, but there's no turning back!

Driftwood Thoughts Among the Pines

Beneath the pines, where shadows play,
Driftwood debates whether to stay.
A log with wisdom shouts out loud,
"Let's gather 'round, it's time to be proud!"

The pebbles chime in, "We're part of the team!"
"We've weathered the storms, we're living the dream!"
A chipmunk sketches their life on a stone,
While the sun winks down, "You're never alone."

As laughter echoes, the trees start to sway,
Breeze tickles leaves in a knotty ballet.
Each twig has a story, each leaf a joke,
In this woodland town, where the wise woodfolk poke.

With driftwood thoughts that drift and glide,
The forest is boisterous, warm, and wide.
So bring your best giggles, your quirkiest cheer,
In this leafy realm, it's always sincere!

Twilight's Invitation to Wonder

As twilight whispers with a chuckle and twirl,
The stars peek through, ready to unfurl.
A firefly hosts a party in the dark,
While the moon plays the DJ, in a luminous arc.

The crickets align for a symphonic show,
"Who can chirp loudest? Let's see how we flow!"
The owls hoot backup, with rhythm divine,
While shadows boogie, no need to refine.

In the twinkling hush, imagination blooms,
As woodland critters dance in cozy rooms.
Under canopies sprinkled with starlight's gleam,
Each laugh and twirl sparks a beautiful dream.

So join the gala, let worries take flight,
In dusk's gentle hand, everything feels right.
With a flick of a wing and a snicker or two,
Twilight beckons us, "Come play, it's all new!"

Labyrinths of Life in the Great Outdoors

In the woods, I twirl and spin,
Chasing squirrels, for the win!
Branches wave like silly flags,
Nature's dance, it never drags.

A path appears, then fades away,
Was that a bird or loud toupee?
I trip on roots, my shoes are stuck,
Why's the trail a game of luck?

Thorns and brambles, all in sight,
A hedge maze on a rainy night.
I shout for help, a friendly bear,
But he just snuggles with my hair.

I laugh at shadows, giggle loud,
This nature's circus is quite the crowd!
With every twist, a funny tale,
Through this green funhouse, I will sail.

The Haunting of the Timbered Realm

In eerie woods, a ghost did prance,
With twiggy legs, it led a dance.
I waved hello, it winked at me,
Then vanished with a rustling spree.

A tree stump spoke in whispered tones,
It said, 'I miss my old cell phones!'
Each leaf a rascal in disguise,
Giggling softly as it flies.

I swear I saw a gnarled tree,
Try to trip a busy bee.
With laughter echoing through the pines,
I joined the fun, ignoring signs.

The chipmunks chuckled, oh what a scene,
As shadows danced, they fit the theme.
'Tis a haunted place, just not the same,
Where laughter's ghost plays silly games.

Icarus Among the Green Shadows

With wings of wax, I soar too high,
But who knew trees could make me cry?
A branch snagged my feathery dream,
Down I tumbled, a nature theme.

The bushes giggled, mocking my fall,
'Did you think you wouldn't hit a wall?'
The sky looked down with frowning sparks,
As birds laughed from their lofty parks.

I landed softly on a nest,
With plump little birds, I felt blessed.
They taught me how to strut and sway,
Who needed wings? I'd fly this way!

So here I frolic, near the green,
Among the leaves, I reign as queen!
Forget the skies, this ground is swell,
In shadows deep, I'll weave my spell.

A Poetic Passage Through Nature's Closet

In nature's closet, what do I see?
A colorful hat and a grumpy bee.
Old boots that squeak as I take a stroll,
And a jacket that swallows my whole.

There's a hanging scarf, wooly and bright,
It flutters about, giving me fright.
A talking tree says, 'What's your style?'
I shrug and laugh, it's been a while.

Mismatched gloves in pairs of three,
The squirrels dart and giggle with glee.
They wear my socks, those furry thieves,
While I contemplate fashion leaves!

With laughter echoing on the breeze,
I dance in circles, just do as I please.
In this closet of fun, I've found my gear,
Who needs a runway? Nature's near!

www.ingramcontent.com/pod-product-compliance
Lightning Source LLC
Chambersburg PA
CBHW071849160426
43209CB00003B/476